Gold Rush NEWS

by Cynthia Benjamin
illustrated by Nick Harris

Harcourt

Orlando   Boston   Dallas   Chicago   San Diego

Visit *The Learning Site!*

www.harcourtschool.com

Gold Found at Sutter's Mill
June 1, 1848

John Sutter

Gold was discovered at Sutter's sawmill on the American River in January of this year. John Sutter owns the sawmill and the land around it. He came to the United States from Switzerland and moved to California in 1839.

Mr. Sutter is a real adventurer. The Mexican government gave him 50,000 acres of land in the Sacramento Valley. Farming and trade made him rich. He built Fort Sutter near the Sacramento River. The fort has shops, a flour mill, a blanket factory, and rooms for his workers and guests.

James Marshall first discovered the gold. Sutter had hired Marshall to build a sawmill about 45 miles east of the fort. Mr. Marshall went to work at the sawmill one day. To his amazement he noticed a yellow metal shining in some water.

Mr. Marshall said, "I thought it was gold, but I tested it to be sure. I banged the metal with a stone. It didn't break into small pieces." Right away, Marshall rode back to the fort to show the gold to his boss.

Sutter wanted to keep the discovery a secret. "I didn't want gold miners running all over my land," he said. He even made his mill workers agree not to talk about the discovery.

It was impossible to keep the news a secret, however. Finding gold is too profitable a discovery.

Sutter's sawmill on the American River

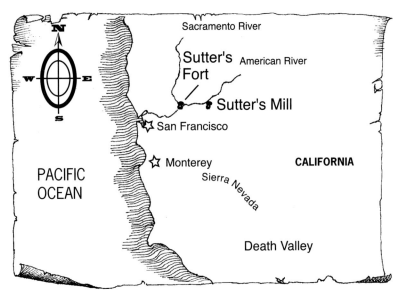

Location of Sutter's Mill

Soon the workers at Mr. Sutter's mill were looking for gold after work. Even Mr. Sutter talked about the gold in a letter to a neighbor.

Then the news spread to San Francisco. At first no one paid much attention. However, a newspaper owner went to Sutter's mill to check out the story. When he returned, he ran through the streets with a bottle filled with gold dust. "Gold beckons," he cried. "You must answer its call and search for it."

Beginning in May San Francisco went crazy. Everyone left town to look for gold. That's why we're calling this newspaper the *Gold Rush News*.

The Ship *California* Reaches San Francisco
February 28, 1849

Today the United States ship the *California* arrived in San Francisco. Its passengers came to California to look for gold. They traveled by sea because it's the fastest route to the gold fields. Unfortunately, it's also very expensive. Most of the travelers started their journey in Boston or New York. They traveled south to Panama and landed in a port on the Atlantic Ocean. Then they went across Panama to reach Panama City on the Pacific Ocean. There they boarded the *California* for the last part of their journey.

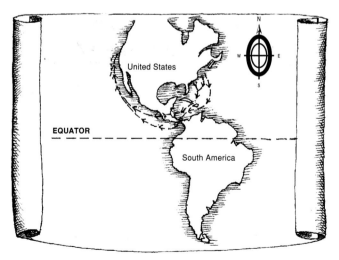

Sea route to California

Several passengers from the *California* were interviewed for this article. One of them was James Lawrence, a teacher from Philadelphia.

"I found it difficult to reserve space on the ship when it left New York," Mr. Lawrence said. "Thousands of people were anxious to travel to Panama so they could reach California quickly. However, there was only room on the ship for 250 passengers. The lucky ones happily paid their fares."

Mr. Lawrence found the voyage very difficult. "The ship was very crowded. The Atlantic Ocean was rough. There were several terrible storms along the way. I slept in a small cabin with fourteen other passengers. We couldn't even sit up. Other people were even more unfortunate. They slept on long wooden shelves that were 6 feet long and 18 inches wide. Some passengers slept in the lifeboats."

When the passengers arrived in Panama, they had to travel in small boats to reach another town. After the boat trip, the travelers had to journey 25 miles through the jungles of Panama on mules and horses. The narrow trail was rough and muddy. Many passengers became ill from yellow fever.

Another passenger, Mildred Lewis, described waiting in Panama City for the steamship *California*.

"Because of the gold rush, there were thousands of travelers waiting for a ship to take them to San Francisco. Some of them had been there for months. When the *California* arrived, everyone rushed to buy a ticket. There was only room for 250 passengers. However, by the time the steamship left port, 365 passengers were on board.

"Because there were too many people, the ship ran out of food and fuel. When the ship finally reached San Francisco, the crew left the ship. All of them wanted to look for gold, too!"

Passengers boarding the *California* in Panama City

A wagon train with fifty people arrived in our town Thursday morning. The group had left Independence, Missouri, five months ago on the 2,000-mile journey. As soon as they arrived, the travelers purchased supplies at the general store here. All of them had stories to tell about their trip on the overland route to California.

The group followed routes that had been used by fur traders before the gold rush began. The maps used by the traders were helpful. Unfortunately, the maps didn't include information about the heat during the day and the cold at night.

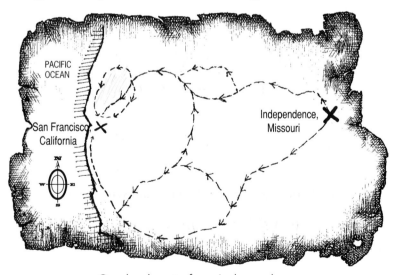

Overland route from Independence, Missouri, to San Francisco, California

A covered wagon on a ferry, crossing the Missouri River

If the dust, rainstorms, and hunger weren't enough, there was another enemy. A terrible illness called cholera hit Missouri just when the wagon train started its journey. Almost twenty people died on the trip. Others returned to their homes in the East rather than continue the journey.

Robert Brown was the leader of this wagon train. He described how hard it was to cross the Missouri River by ferry. "We had to find a ferry crossing that wasn't crowded. I saw one ferry sink. The man steering it drowned. It was a sad sight."

Wagon train traveling across the prairie

Many of the people on the wagon train weren't farmers. As a result they didn't know how to handle the horses, cows, and mules on the long journey. Also, the rugged trails were often difficult to travel on. When these unskilled people decided to hunt buffaloes, the wounded animals attacked them.

The inexperienced travelers faced another problem. They had brought too many things with them. Items such as furniture and tools made the wagons too heavy for the horses. The travelers had to abandon many things along the route. They were all glad when they finally reached Gold Creek at the end of their trip.

Miners Find Gold!
October 10, 1849

Late this afternoon two miners ran into town carrying bags of gold. They discovered the gold along the western hills of the Sierra Nevada. The miners, Mike Daley and Leo Jones, had been digging for only a month. They had used picks and shovels to dig in the dirt near the mining camp.

"You can call it hard work," said Mike Daley, pointing to the bags of gold, "or you can call it luck. I think it's a bit of both."

Mike Daley and Leo Jones with some of the gold they discovered

His partner disagreed. "We've been living in a tent for a month. It's freezing at night. Just last week we had to fight off a bear that came into camp. Luck had nothing to do with it."

Bill Russell panning for gold

Mike Daley and Leo Jones are the only miners who have found gold lately. Many have come back from the mining camps with nothing.

"I've been looking for gold about 15 miles outside of town," said Bill Russell. He was a teacher in Philadelphia before coming to California. "I don't have enough money for a shovel. I've been using a gold pan to look for gold in the river. It was a tub my mother used to wash clothes in. I put some dirt and water in the tub. Then I shake it from side to side. Any gold dust or pieces of gold will sink to the bottom."

Worry About High Prices
November 1, 1849

Miners must pay high prices for food and supplies. Some merchants take supplies to mining camps and sell them directly to the occupants of the tents, shacks, and log cabins. There are also stores in towns near the places where miners dig for gold. In every case miners must pay very high prices for the simplest food.

One miner spent $15.00 for a jar of pickles and two sweet potatoes. Another miner, Jim Clark, paid $7.50 for a needle and thread. An ounce of gold is worth $16.00. Miners must strike it rich to afford to eat. Because of the high prices for goods, many miners can't buy fresh fruit and vegetables.

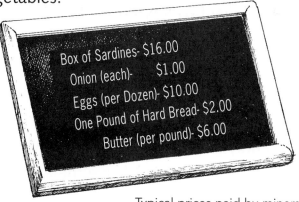

Box of Sardines- $16.00
Onion (each)- $1.00
Eggs (per Dozen)- $10.00
One Pound of Hard Bread- $2.00
Butter (per pound)- $6.00

Typical prices paid by miners

Gold Miners Disagree About Claim
November 5, 1849

John Monroe at his claim

John Monroe said that another miner, Howard Davis, tried to steal his claim. Monroe had been digging near Red Creek when he found gold there. He left his tools next to the area where he had been digging. This is one way of holding a claim. Then he went to town to buy supplies. When he came back two days later, he found Howard Davis digging for gold on his claim. Monroe went to the claims officer of the mining camp. The officer, Mark Petersen, said that Mr. Monroe had only left his claim for two days. To give up a claim, a miner must leave the area for a week.

14

Flood Strikes Sacramento!
January 10, 1850

A great flood has turned Sacramento into a sea of water and mud. The flood was caused by heavy rains that began late last year. The flood waters swept into the town, which is near the Sacramento River. Citizens climbed onto roofs or clung to pieces of wood or broken trees. Boats rescued the lucky ones. Less fortunate people drowned. Now that the flood waters are starting to dry up, there's another problem—mud. Sacramento has turned into a giant mud hole.

Miners and merchants depend on supplies bought in Sacramento. The town must be cleaned up and rebuilt quickly.

A flooded street in Sacramento

Our Town Has A Birthday!
April 10, 1850

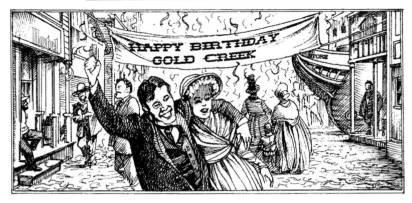

Gold Creek citizens celebrating

Gold Creek was founded one year ago today by gold miners. Today the citizens of our good town got together for a big party. There was dancing in the streets and a special picnic supper. The children played games and joined in the dancing.

We are all proud of how much Gold Creek has grown in just one year. When the miners first arrived, they lived in tents and shacks. In time two-story buildings made of brick were built. Now we have hotels, stores, and restaurants. Some of them were built from wood and other materials taken from abandoned ships. We have citizens from Europe, Mexico, and Australia. Our growing town is truly multicultural.